ANKYLOSAURUS

AND OTHER MOUNTAIN DINOSAURS

by **Dougal Dixon**

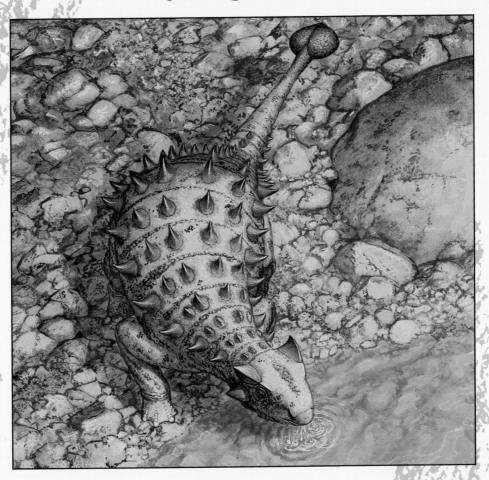

illustrated by
Steve Weston and James Field

PICTURE WINDOW BOOKS
Minneapolis, Minnesota

Picture Window Books
5115 Excelsior Boulevard
Suite 232
Minneapolis, MN 55416
877-845-8392
www.picturewindowbooks.com

Printed in the United States of America.

Library of Congress Cataloging-in-Publication Data
Dixon, Dougal.
Ankylosaurus and other mountain dinosaurs /
written by Dougal Dixon ; illustrations by James Field,
Steve Weston ; diagrams by Stefan Chabluk ; cover
art by Steve Weston.
p. cm. — (Dinosaur find)
Includes bibliographical references and index.
ISBN 1-4048-0670-9
1. Dinosaurs—Juvenile literature. 2. Mountain
animals—Juvenile literature. I. Field, James, 1959- ill.
II. Weston, Steve, ill. III. Chabluk, Stefan, ill. IV. Title.
QE861.5.D34 2005
567.9—dc22   2004007304

Acknowledgments
This book was produced for Picture Window Books
by Bender Richardson White, U.K.

Illustrations by James Field (pages 4–5, 7, 11, 15)
and Steve Weston (cover and pages 9, 13, 17, 19,
21). Diagrams by Stefan Chabluk.
Photograph copyrights: Corbis Images, pages 6, 8
(Robert Gill/Papilio),12 (Joe McDonald), and 20.
Digital Vision, pages 10, 14, 16, and 18.

Consultant: John Stidworthy, Scientific Fellow of
the Zoological Society, London, and former
Lecturer in the Education Department, Natural
History Museum, London.

Reading Adviser: Rosemary G. Palmer, Ph.D.,
Department of Literacy, College of Education,
Boise State University, Idaho

Types of dinosaurs
In this book, a red shape at the top of a left-hand page shows the animal was a meat-eater. A green shape shows it was a plant-eater.

Just how big—or small—were they?
Dinosaurs were many different sizes. We have compared their size to one of the following:

Chicken
2 feet (60 cm) tall
Weight 6 pounds (2.7 kg)

Adult person
6 feet (1.8 m) tall
Weight 170 pounds (76.5 kg)

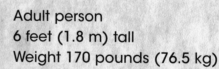

Elephant
10 feet (3 m) tall
Weight 12,000 pounds
(5,400 kg)

TABLE OF CONTENTS

WHAT'S INSIDE?

Dinosaurs! These dinosaurs lived in hills, mountains, or in the valleys between them. Find out how they survived millions of years ago and what they have in common with today's animals.

LIFE IN THE MOUNTAINS

Dinosaurs lived between 230 million and 65 million years ago. The land and seas were not in the same places then. Many dinosaurs lived on hills and mountains or in the valleys between them.

Ankylosaurus and *Stegoceras* lived in the mountains. When it was warm, many animals lived near the top of the mountains. When it got cold, they lived near the bottom in the valleys.

5

AMARGASAURUS
Pronunciation: uh-MAR-guh-SAW-rus

Amargasaurus had big spines down its long neck. They used these spines for signaling to one another. If the herd stayed together, they would all be safer.

On the move today

Wildebeest travel in herds just like *Amargasaurus* did long ago.

Size Comparison

Amargasaurus walked the hills looking for plants. Their waving spines made them look like a moving forest.

ANCHISAURUS

Pronunciation:
ANG-ki-SAW-rus

Anchisaurus had large eyes and sharp teeth. Its teeth snipped leaves off plants. *Anchisaurus* could also have stood on its back legs to reach leaves high up on bushes. It used its long neck to reach food among rocks.

Reaching up today

Antelope often stand up on their back legs to eat like *Anchisaurus* did.

Size Comparison

An *Anchisaurus* would look down on the valley from a hilltop. It was looking for ferns and bushes to eat.

Almost nothing that lived in the hills could hurt *Ankylosaurus*. Its back was covered with armor. Even its eyelids had armor. *Ankylosaurus* also had a heavy club on its tail. It used this to fight its enemies.

Protective armor today

The thick skin of an Indian rhinoceros acts like armor and protects it. The armor of an *Ankylosaurus* did the same thing.

Size Comparison

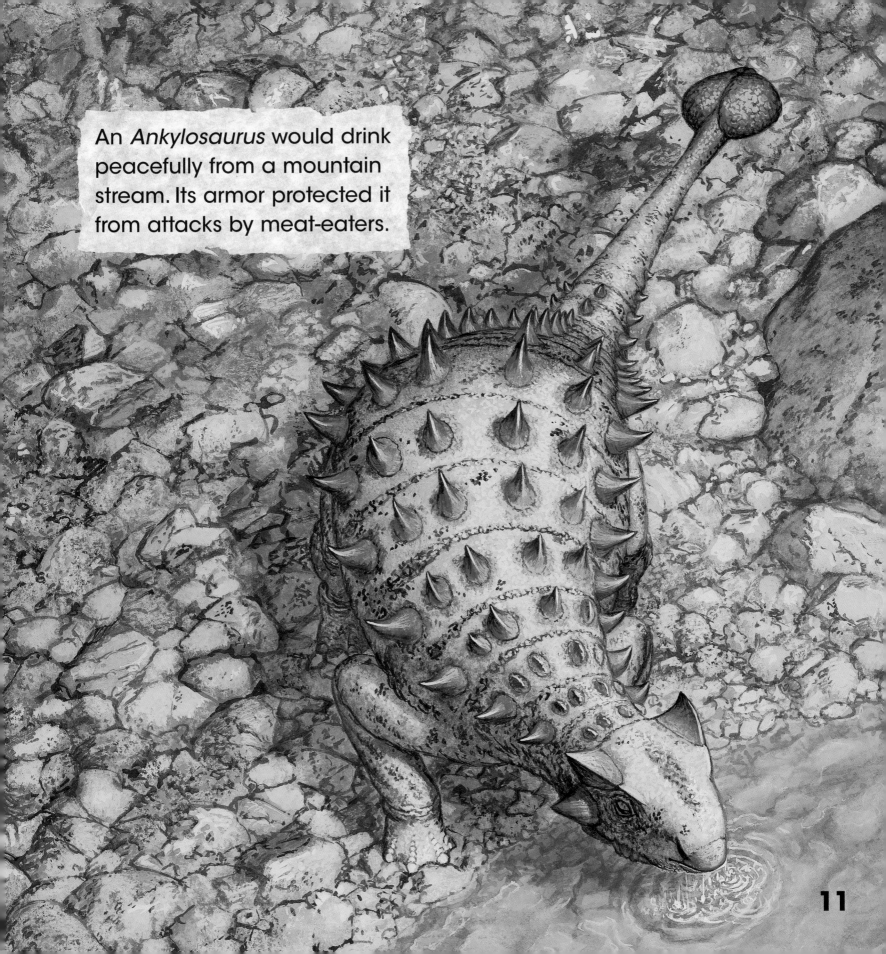

An *Ankylosaurus* would drink peacefully from a mountain stream. Its armor protected it from attacks by meat-eaters.

11

Eoraptor was a hunter. It had long back legs and was a fast runner. It chased after little animals like rat-sized mammals, insects, and lizards. The dark colors on its back helped it hide among the rocks.

Fast feet today

Roadrunners use their long, strong legs to chase after little animals like *Eoraptor* did millions of years ago.

Size Comparison

A hungry *Eoraptor* raced between trees after a small mammal.

13

Herrerasaurus moved through the uplands on strong back feet. It had huge jaws for catching food to eat. Its sharp teeth were like knives. They were used for tearing up meat.

Big eater today

A crocodile tears huge pieces of meat off its dinner. It swallows big pieces of meat like *Herrerasaurus* once did.

Size Comparison

An *Herrerasaurus*
ripped the meat
off a dead reptile.

15

SCELIDOSAURUS

Pronunciation:
skel-EYE-doe-SAW-rus

Scelidosaurus lived in the forested hills. It held its head close to the ground. *Scelidosaurus* ate short ferns with its beak. Its bony spikes helped it stay safe from meat-eaters. Its spiky shape also helped it hide among plants.

Protective spikes today

The horny devil lizard is all spiky like *Scelidosaurus* was. Sharp scales don't make a good meal.

Size Comparison

16

A heavy *Scelidosaurus* would walk slowly between the rocks. Its armor was its only protection.

SCUTELLOSAURUS

Pronunciation:
skoo-TELL-o-SAW-rus

Scutellosaurus was covered with little armor plates. It had more than 300 bony spikes on its back. It ate plants and looked like a lizard. Maybe it sat in the sun to warm up. Then it could have hidden under rocks to cool off.

Rolling up today

Some lizards have spikes on their back like *Scutellosaurus* did. A few lizards roll into a ball when attacked.

Size Comparison

A *Scutellosaurus* watched for danger. It could run away from meat-eaters. It could also curl up into a ball. Then its armor would protect it.

19

Stegoceras had thick bone plates on top of their heads. They fought by crashing their heads together. The fights showed who would lead the herd. *Stegoceras* also had narrow feet that helped them walk on rocky ground.

Banging heads today

Bighorn rams often have head-butting fights like *Stegoceras* did long ago.

Size Comparison

Two *Stegoceras* charged into one another. They fought to see which was stronger.

21

WHERE DID THEY GO?

Dinosaurs are extinct, which means that none of them are alive today. Scientists study rocks and fossils to find clues about what happened to dinosaurs.

People have different explanations about what happened. Some people think a huge asteroid that hit Earth caused all sorts of climate changes. This then caused the dinosaurs to die. Others think volcanic eruptions caused the climate to change and that killed the dinosaurs. No one knows for sure, though.

Glossary

beak—the hard front part of the mouth of birds and some dinosaurs

ferns—plants with finely divided leaves known as fronds; ferns are common in damp woods and on mountains

herd—a large group of animals that move, feed, and sleep together

insects—small, six-legged animals; they include ants, bees, beetles, and flies

mammals—warm-blooded animals that have hair and drink mother's milk when they are young; today's mammals include cats, dogs, rabbits, mice, bears, monkeys, and humans

reptile—a cold-blooded animal with a backbone and scales; it walks on short legs or crawls on its belly

signaling—making a sign, warning, or hint

upland—any high ground

FIND OUT MORE

AT THE LIBRARY

Dixon, Dougal. *Dougal Dixon's Dinosaurs.* Honesdale, Pa.: Boyds Mills Press, 1998.

Lessem, Don. *The Deadliest Dinosaurs.* Minneapolis: Lerner, 2005.

Oliver, Rupert. *Ankylosaurus.* Vero Beach, Fla.: Rourke Publishing, 2001.

ON THE WEB

FactHound offers a safe, fun way to find Web sites related to this book. All of the sites on FactHound have been researched by our staff.

1. Visit *www.facthound.com*

2. Type in this special code: 1404806709

3. Click on the FETCH IT button.

Your trusty FactHound will fetch the best Web sites for you!

LOOK FOR ALL OF THE BOOKS IN THE DINOSAUR FIND SERIES:

INDEX